BY THE EDITORS OF CONSUMER GUIDE®

BIG TRUCKS

Bell Publishing Company
New York

CONTENTS

Library of Congress Catalog Card Number: 77-94001

This edition published by.
Bell Publishing Company
A Division of Crown Publishers, Inc.
One Park Avenue
New York, N.Y. 10016
By arrangement with Publications International, Ltd.

a   b   c   d   e   f   g   h

INTRODUCTION

The 20th century was drawing near; the 1800s were almost gone. It was a time in America when milk, blocks of ice to keep it cool, and all other goods were being carted around the cities by horse-drawn wagons; when farmers used mules and oxen to plow their fields and horses to haul the produce to market; when cowboys still rode horses to herd their cattle to slaughter; when timber from the nation's great forests was dragged out by beasts of burden. There had to be a better way.

The automobile had just invaded the American scene. But as the year 1900 approached, a number of companies and individuals were already at their drawing boards, modifying the newfangled invention to handle the growing needs of commerce. Soon, a menagerie of strange-looking motorized carts and wagons began to appear on the unpaved roads of the United States.

In 1899, Autocar brought out its first truck. The following year, White and Mack introduced theirs.

Ford trucks were already hard at work in a variety of configurations by the 1920s.

After that, trucks were turned out by Rapid in 1902, Reo in 1904 and Ford in 1905. Between then and the start of World War I, a period that is often called the "experimental age" of the truck, a number of other important newcomers entered the field: International Harvester, Diamond T, FWD, Oshkosh and Walter.

The first trucks were really horseless buggies with platforms extending out behind them. As barrels, crates and other items continued to slide off them on hills or in the mud, the truck industry devised rails to keep the payload on the truck and vans to protect the cargo from the elements.

World War I created an urgent demand for trucks, and the industry met the challenge. General John J. Pershing, who had carefully looked over the situation in Europe, said he would need a minimum of 50,000 trucks immediately. American truck manufacturers turned out 230,000 military vehicles in 1918 to help the general. Since then, trucks carrying troops, equipment, food, medical supplies and other military necessities have been a welcome sight to the American fighting man on the battlefields of Europe and the South Pacific, the deserts of North Africa, the frozen hills of Korea and the jungles of Vietnam.

Industry and commerce in the 1930s adopted the truck and put it to work in a variety of ways. It rounded out the transportation network, augmenting the railroads that could go only where the rails took them and the ships that were confined to the waterways.

Trucks traveled the city streets and alleys, handling all the public and private hauling jobs. Huge tractors appeared on the open highways, pulling long trailers and tall trailers, open and enclosed trailers, double trailers and triple ones. And when the government restricted the length of trucks, the industry ingeniously devised the cab-over-engine

Mack stake truck, vintage 1926.

By 1930, General Motors was marketing a variety of trucks for use in delivery and construction.

tractor: the cab was shortened, but not the trailer carrying the cargo. Conventional cabs are designed with the driver's compartment set back of the engine, like an automobile. A system of classifying trucks according to their size and hauling power was developed. Class 8 trucks are biggest of all.

Huge trucks were equipped with refrigerated vans to keep food and other perishables fresh. Tankers were devised to move oil, chemicals, gasoline and milk. Open trucks instead of cowboys delivered livestock, and automobiles were carried piggy-back from the factory to the dealer. Dynamite and other explosives were hauled on some trucks, household furniture on others.

Giant companies bought fleets of trucks for their own particular purposes. Individuals bought a tractor/trailer and went into business on their own. The trucker became a folk hero, visible on the highway in all climates and under all conditions, and was heard talking a language all his own on CB radios.

It is often easy to take for granted everything that trucks and truckers provide today. But stop and think for a moment about the roast on tonight's dinner menu. A rancher used a truck to bring his steer to auction, another huge truck hauled that steer and 50 others to the slaughterhouse, and a third big rig carried the processed beef to the supermarket. And we cannot forget about the leftovers we don't eat and the wrappings the roast came in: they'll leave in a refuse disposal truck.

It is all very necessary, but it is also exciting. Trucking has a glamour all its own. The rigs are often as beautiful as they are powerful. To see them up close, to hear and feel the rumble of their great engines and to watch as they move off down the highway is to be touched by the American Spirit.

Mack delivery truck of 1936.

Freightliner cab-over-engine from 1950.

CHEVROLET

There once was a man named Louis Chevrolet, who attached his name to a line of automobiles that was to become one of the most famous and successful makes in the world. His company became part of General Motors and helped that corporation to become one of the wealthiest in industrial history.

It would seem, considering the tremendous popularity of the Chevrolet automobile, that Chevrolet's name would have been a byword for many years in truck manufacturing as well. Not so: Chevy trucks are new on the scene, having split from the GMC line only eight years ago.

Today, Chevy offers a variety of truck models to challenge any company in the heavy-duty hauling field. Chevy trucks are available in cab-over-engine models as well as conventional models. Heavy trucks are offered for long-distance hauling; mediums are made by Chevrolet for lighter loads and shorter trips.

The Chevy Bison is a conventional model. It is the result of five years of planning and testing. Chevrolet calls it "the magnificent beast" because it is one of the toughest high-performance vehicles on the road today. Engines for the Bison range from 219 to 412 horsepower diesels, and are available in either turbocharged or naturally aspirated models. Adaptable to a variety of heavy hauling purposes, the Bison is the running mate of Chevy's cab-over-engine model, the Titan.

The Titan is a long-distance hauler which could be termed a lightweight COE. It offers a choice of 17 different diesel engines, and the cab is designed with all the comfort and convenience consid-

Chevrolet Bison hauls a heavy load of sand to a construction site.

Chevrolet Bison with van trailer.

Chevrolet Series 90 diesel.

erations that are important to the cross-country trucker. Available with the Titan is an optional "Dragfoiler," a molded fiberglass foil that has been aerodynamically designed to fit the top of the cab and cut down wind resistance.

For both the Titan and the Bison, Chevy offers one of the largest packages of optional accessories presently available. Fuel economy is a prime concern with Chevy trucks. Powertrains incorporate what Chevy calls "fuel-squeezer" engines and the

Side-by-side comparison of the 1978 Chevrolet Bruin (left) and Series 70 shows difference in size.

Many Chevrolet CE65 trucks are equipped with tanker bodies for hauling liquids.

appropriate six-, seven- and nine-speed manual and automatic transmissions.

The Chevy Bruin is a newcomer to the line of heavy-duty workers. The Bruin is a conventional model, short but powerful and with an exceptionally wide windshield for good visibility.

Chevy also makes a complete line of medium trucks to serve all types of city and construction-site functions. They are also used as tankers and farm vehicles. Turbocharged diesel engines are available for the mediums, and the various styles and models serve practically all needs in this area of truck transportation.

Chevy has a vast network of dealers and service facilities throughout the United States. Like Louis Chevrolet's cars, the trucks that bear his name have come to play a major role in American transportation.

Chevrolet D90 Series Titan.

Chevrolet Series 90 conventional cab.

CRANE CARRIER CORPORATION (CCC)

Crane Carrier Corporation began, as its name suggests, with a line of trucks that carried cranes. The single aim of the company's founders in 1946 was to rebuild surplus military vehicles, adapting them to transport cranes and drilling rigs. That activity was successful for a time, but then the supply of surplus trucks began to dwindle. Company managers realized that to remain alive and well, CCC would have to stop searching for surplus trucks and start manufacturing its own.

Looking at the company today, it is difficult to believe that it did not gear up for truck manufacturing until 1953. CCC still specializes in the production of heavy-duty mobile cranes and carriers for drilling equipment, but it has also branched out into the building of trucks for a wide range of other functions. Presently, CCC has an entire stable of models, including vehicles used by logging, mining, petroleum exploration and interstate shipping companies. It all began with an investment of $5000; today, Crane Carrier's annual sales top $77 million.

One of the newest members of the Crane Carrier line is the Centurion, a rugged, efficient refuse hauler that incorporates many advanced features. One of the truck's innovations is its ability to accommodate all types of refuse hauling bodies without any modification of the carrier's chassis. The Centurion series comes in a variety of models to fit individual needs. It is a cab-over-engine type, powered by a six-cylinder diesel engine. Inside the cab, its wraparound console puts all controls within easy reach of the operator. It is noted for the excellent visibility it provides.

Crane Carrier's Century is designed to meet the needs of concrete suppliers and the construction industry.

Crane Carrier Centaur chassis.

CCC truck equipped with post-hole drill.

Crane Carrier Centurion chassis.

Crane Carrier Centaur dump truck.

CCC Centurion with tanker.

CCC Centaur with dump trailer.

Another group of cab-over-engine CCC trucks, the Century series, serves the needs of concrete suppliers. These powerful trucks feature a one-man offset cab with wraparound windshield for increased visibility. Powerful and versatile, the Century can carry concrete mixers over the highway or across the rugged terrain of construction sites. It can be customized to handle a variety of materials and can be used as a dump truck.

CCC's Centaur series, named for the famous mythological creatures that were half man and half horse, is a line of conventional-cab workhorses engineered for hauling both on and off the highway. The new line has proved itself on America's roads and in the oil fields, as well as at the construction sites and logging camps where it was first tested. Centaurs are also widely used overseas. Extra strong and powered by a six-cylinder, turbocharged diesel engine, the Centaur can accommodate both van and dump trailer configurations.

Crane Carrier Corporation, headquartered in Tulsa, Oklahoma, also maintains 16 parts and component depots in ten other states and in Canada. The main assembly plant for CCC in Tulsa is a modern giant, 500,000 square feet in area. In a short 25 years, Crane Carrier Corporation has established itself as one of the very important names in the field of heavy truck manufacture.

FORD

There are few names that have been more closely associated with motorized transportation than Henry Ford's. His name has been affixed to hundreds of millions of vehicles over the years. Ford Motor Company is now the third largest industrial corporation in the United States, one that grosses more than $28 billion a year.

Considering Ford's pioneering work with the passenger car, it is not surprising to hear that Ford also built one of the first trucks ever made. What is surprising is that Henry Ford put the truck together three years before Ford Motor Company existed

and 17 years before a Ford Motor Company truck rolled off the assembly line.

It was in 1900, while Ford was working for the Detroit Auto Company, that he designed and built a panel-type delivery truck. It did not go into production then. During the next decade, with Ford now in charge of his own automotive company and trucks becoming a more common sight on America's roads, Ford Motor Company designers were working on a model of their own. That truck did not see mass production until 1917. Called the Ford TT, it was a Model T passenger car with a one-ton truck

New in Ford's big-truck lineup is the CL-9000, a heavy-duty diesel with cab-over-engine design.

chassis. As the truck manufacturing industry grew, so too did Ford's efforts in the field. The company introduced the first low-priced V8-engine trucks in 1932, and they helped significantly to expand the U.S. truck industry.

World War II forced the company to redirect its operations, and it did so on an incredibly large scale. From 1941 through 1945, Ford turned out a vast array of trucks, four-wheel-drive vehicles, Sherman tanks, armored personnel carriers, amphibious landing craft, B-24 bombers, airplane engines and other military equipment.

After the war, it was back to automobiles and trucks. From that point on, it was a matter of introducing line after line of new trucks. Ford, as a result, can claim to be the largest manufacturer of combined heavy-duty and medium-size trucks in the United States. Ford Motor Company has actually been controlling 27 to 28 percent of the entire market for heavies and mediums in recent years. (GMC and International Harvester are close be-

hind.) Ford today carries six series of trucks in the heavy/medium classification, and sells more than 87,000 of them each year.

Ford calls its CL-9000 "the biggest, boldest cab-over-engine linehaul diesel truck ever developed by the Ford Motor Company." Inside the aluminum cab are nearly all the comforts of home: the truck is designed for the long-distance driver who will have to spend many hours behind the wheel and a number of days and nights in the truck. The CL-9000 can be adapted to haul a variety of payloads.

The Ford W series is another group of rugged linehaul COE tractors, geared for the open road and capable of moving raw timber on a flatbed or finished furniture in a van. The W-9000 is available in 118- and 134-inch wheelbases; the WT-9000 in wheelbases of 142, 152 and 164 inches.

In the "Louisville" or L series of conventional Ford trucks which was introduced in 1970, there are actually two sub-series. The 600 through 800

Ford L-600 medium-duty truck.

Ford W-9000 cab-over rig.

Ford L-9000 conventional cab.

Ford C-750 medium-duty truck.

Ford's LTL-9000, an over-the-road hauler, comes with a comfortable sleeping compartment for overnight trips.

models are mediums for construction work, farming and intercity hauling. The L-900, L-8000 and L-9000 compose a group of larger trucks for such duties as logging, refuse disposal and transport of concrete mixers.

Ford's F series is its best-seller in the medium field. There are seven models in the series, offering nine different wheelbases. These light but rugged vehicles are used for a variety of urban, suburban and farm chores.

An intermediate truck—somewhere between heavy and medium—is the Ford C series. It is used to transport fuel in tanks, solid waste in compactors and freight in vans.

Ford is the biggest name in the hotly competitive heavy-duty and medium truck business. More than 275 dealers sell and service Ford's trucks. New trucks are on the drawing board, and refinements are planned for the trucks already on the road. Ford is determined to stay in the top spot.

Ford L-600 medium-duty truck.

Ford F-600 with stretched cab.

FREIGHTLINER

The launching of Freightliner trucks was a case of bad timing. The year was 1939 when the established firm of Consolidated Freightways in Salt Lake City, Utah, decided to bring out a line of heavy-duty trucks. But in that year, much of the world went to war. As the very first Freightliner trucks rolled out of the plant and onto America's highways, the United States entered World War II. The company's operations came to an abrupt halt.

The war ended in 1945, but Americans spent most of the following year trying to get back on their feet. Of the companies that had been shut down because of the war, many were never able to open their doors again. Consolidated Freightways did reopen in 1947, with a plant in Portland, Ore-gon, and began producing a line of big diesel trucks. The company started with only $60,000 in capital and little fanfare. Five full-time employees worked in a small, rented warehouse. Freightliner moved ahead, eventually establishing itself as a viable part of the truck building industry.

The company, a specialist in the industry, has one major goal: to custom-build dependable Class 8 trucks for fleets and independent owner/operators. Its beginning may have been ill-timed, but the company did get started on the right foot in building an enviable reputation: the very first truck Freightliner ever sold ran for more than four million miles before it was honorably retired from service.

In 1951, Freightliner and White Motor Corpo-

The lineup from Freightliner includes both conventional (left) and cab-over-engine rigs with comfortable sleepers.

Freightliner from the 1950s.

priate, because it was Freightliner that introduced such important developments as the cab-over-engine tractor design, the sleeper unit, the all-aluminum cab and the 90-degree tilt cab. The company can be credited with many contributions to the trucking industry.

Freightliner currently builds a line of three basic truck models; however, there are actually nine different truck types available because each model is offered as a single-drive tractor, dual-drive tractor and dual-drive truck.

The first and perhaps still foremost truck in the Freightliner stable is the C.O.E. (cab-over engine), which has racked up billions of miles on the highway. Today, it is as modern as modern can be, complete with a special four-spring suspension system, luxury interiors in both cab and sleeper, and an almost endless list of options.

The Freightliner Conventional is the newest addition to the company's line. It features an aluminum cab and other strong but light materials, a "command post" deluxe dashboard unit and wide latitude for customization.

The Powerliner is heralded as a combination of "brute power and plush environment," another appropriate choice of words: it is powered by a 600-plus horsepower engine and offers an elegant interior of wood-grain paneling and vinyl.

Freightliner is far from the oldest company in the

ration entered into an agreement whereby White, through its many outlets, sold and serviced Freightliner trucks. The arrangement lasted until 1977 when Freightliner decided to market and service its own vehicles.

Innovation and change are words that Freightliner uses to describe its operation. They are appro-

The C.O.E. is Freightliner's principal product.

Conventional model was introduced in 1974.

Conventionals use lightweight materials.

C.O.E. cab tilts forward for servicing.

truck manufacturing business, but it has come a long way since 1939. It is now a multimillion-dollar corporation that has put more than 80,000 heavy-duty trucks on North American roads in the last decade—trucks that have hauled a great variety of consumer goods and industrial materials. The company is still based in Portland, Oregon, and it is still owned by Consolidated Freightways. But Freightliner's payroll has grown from the five people who worked there during the '40s to a work force of more than 3200.

Freightliner manufactures many of its own parts and components such as fuel tanks and electrical harnesses—even its own air conditioners. Plants turn out trucks every week of the year in Portland; Chino, California; Indianapolis, Indiana; and Burnaby, British Columbia. Five other plants and distribution centers in the United States produce Freightliner parts. The company's new dealer network for sales and service is a growing operation, which is supported by a special team of field service representatives.

Aluminum is used extensively in conventional.

Many paint treatments are available.

FWD

The United States Army approached officials of a small automobile manufacturing company in Clintonville, Wisconsin, in 1912 and asked them to produce a 3-ton and a 1-1/2-ton truck for a special test.

Up to that time, the army had always moved on foot, with help from horses and mules to haul artillery and other supplies for a fighting unit. But the military wanted to find out whether trucks would be a better means of getting a fully equipped and armed regiment from one place to another. The test would pit the trucks and their troops against footsoldiers and their pack animals on a grueling "slow march." The trucks would have to grind onward at a steady speed of no more than 2-1/2 miles an hour.

In the summer of that year, the two regiments set out over the same terrain, heading for the same distant destination. The men, horses and mules of the traditional regiment tired and required rest stops; the trucks, of course, did not. A new era in the transport of military troops and equipment had begun.

The truck maker for the army was the FWD Company, named for its four-wheel-drive vehicles. It was four-wheel drive which enabled these trucks to traverse the same rugged landscape as the men and animals of the traditional unit. Because of the success of the test, the pre-World War I army ordered that all the new motor vehicles purchased for the military would have four-wheel drive.

Four-wheel drive and the FWD Corporation of today actually began with the invention of a four-wheel-drive steam automobile by Otto Zachow and William Besserdich in 1908. They built a prototype that year and tried it out in the snow of frigid Wisconsin. The vehicle's unique traction allowed it to go almost anywhere in the worst winter conditions. On January 9, 1909, FWD was founded as a company. That year, FWD manufactured its first

The brawny trucks from FWD feature four-wheel drive, giving them extra traction for high-speed snow removal.

FWD model for use with concrete mixer.

FWD model equipped for military service.

gasoline-powered, four-wheel-drive automobile. It was nicknamed the "Battleship."

After the army's success with four-wheel-drive trucks, FWD decided to branch out into the truck market while continuing to make automobiles. The first commercial FWD truck sold was a three-ton model, bought by a freight hauler in Michigan. The army, however, proved to be FWD's biggest customer in the early days. General John J. Pershing ordered several hundred of the company's trucks for his pursuit of Pancho Villa into Mexico in 1916. FWD produced more than 20,000 of the now-famous Model B Ammunition Carriers, which moved guns, ammo and other supplies across Europe during World War I.

After the war, about 5000 of these Model B trucks were bought as surplus and adapted by state highway departments. These trucks composed the first road and highway maintenance fleets in the United States.

FWD continued to produce automobiles for a while, including some specially built race cars which competed in the Indianapolis 500 during the 1930s. But automobiles were eventually phased out of the FWD line.

The corporation today is in the business of turning out tough four-wheel-drive trucks for a variety of purposes. Snow and ice must be removed from highways and city streets; cranes and other construction equipment must be moved to construction and mining sites; utility vehicles must get through the most fearsome weather conditions. FWD is currently manufacturing trucks to do these jobs well.

The Tractioneer is the chief FWD model. It can be a snow removal vehicle, designed to work effectively in the worst blizzard. It can be adapted to perform an assortment of warm-weather duties including cargo hauling and road maintenance. The

Tractioneer can be outfitted with shovels, drills, snorkel systems and other heavy equipment to serve the needs of fuel, electrical, water and communications utilities. Other Tractioneers are doing what their forerunners did more than 60 years ago: serving the U.S. military. The truck can be purchased with either a gasoline or a diesel engine.

The company is still headquartered in Clintonville, where approximately 530 employees turn out up to 900 FWD vehicles each year for some of the most demanding jobs on and off America's highways and streets.

FWD maintains a museum in its hometown where cars and trucks like the "Battleship," the first FWD commercial truck, the Model B and the FWD racing cars are on display.

Model used with front-discharge mixers.

GMC

No book on the American trucking industry would be complete without a mention of names like Henry Ford, R.E. Olds, Kent and Worthington, White and Walter. These pioneers carved a niche for themselves in history more than half a century ago, and their names can still be seen on trucks rolling off assembly lines today. Among them, of course, we must include the name of Max Grabowski.

His name may not be as well remembered as some of the others, but his contribution to the U.S. trucking industry was a major one.

Grabowski's Rapid Motor Vehicle Company built its first truck in a small shop in Detroit in 1902. In 1904, Rapid moved to a plant in Pontiac, Michigan, and continued building trucks. Four years later, General Motors Company was founded and promptly purchased a majority of Rapid's stock. Rapid and another Michigan truck firm, Reliance Motor Truck Company, were combined by GM in 1911 and called the General Motors Truck Company. Two years after that, Reliance operations were moved to Pontiac, and that city has been the home of GM's truck plant ever since.

Today, GMC Truck and Coach Division of General Motors is one of the Big Three manufacturers in the field of heavy-duty and medium-size trucks, along with Ford and International Harvester. The Big Three control approximately 75 percent of the large-truck market today.

GMC's Astro 95 can be fitted with the company's Dragfoiler to improve mileage by as much as 20 percent.

GMC currently makes almost every kind of truck imaginable, from the enormous tractor/trailer combinations that haul huge loads cross-country to the smallest pickups, campers and vans. In the area of large trucks, the various GMC lines offer trucks to fill the requirements of nearly all channels of industry and commerce.

Among the newest of the GMC trucks is the General. Introduced in 1977, this huge conventional rig is one which GMC regards as its "entry into the elite market of luxury heavy-duty trucks." The General is loaded with many luxuries and conveniences available as standard equipment and others as optional accessories. The welded aluminum cab comes in either of two BBC (bumper to back-of-cab) lengths—108-inch regular and 116-inch tandem. Generals haul everything from bricks to petroleum; from timber to shipments of new General Motors automobiles.

GMC's Astro 95 is the company's cab-over-engine interstate hauler. Three styles are available: a tandem-axle, 86-inch cab; a single-axle, 86-inch cab; and a single-axle, 54-inch cab without sleeper. The Astro 95 is designed to meet and handle all kinds of long-distance hauling needs. Plush interi-

GMC's 6500 short conventional.

ors offer a variety of appointments, including high-back seats and woodgrain, wraparound dashboard consoles. A new Astro SS, added to the line in 1977, was developed especially for the own-

The Brigadier, a heavy-duty conventional model, is the newest truck in the broad GMC lineup.

GMC's huge General conventional.

Series 6500 stake truck.

er/operator. It includes a wide assortment of comfort and appearance features.

For tough over-the-road jobs, the company also produces a line that is adaptable to either tractor or truck applications—the conventional 9500 series. These short conventionals are available in either single-axle or tandem-axle models. According to GMC, they were designed to provide brawn for their assignments and comfort for their operators. The 9500s are among the most adaptable of GMC's heavy-duty trucks.

Another short conventional model is the 7500 series. These trucks also are adaptable to a wide variety of hauling services, from open-highway transport to urban refuse disposal. The 7500s can be obtained with either diesel or gasoline engines.

The GMC 6500 series provides the owner with a

6500 equipped for intercity deliveries.

choice of either a conventional model or the new Steel Tilt, a cab-over-engine style. These medium trucks have already proved themselves in many different kinds of highway and urban hauling jobs.

The 5000 series and the 6000 series are geared to handle smaller chores than those taken on by the other GMC heavies and mediums. But these conventionals are still rugged and durable, and they are especially practical for city and suburban uses. The 5000s and 6000s are highly maneuverable vehicles, and are engineered to withstand the long periods of idling and stop-and-go driving that is so common.

GMC does not manufacture its own powerplants. Instead, it calls upon other General Motors divisions for two of the engines. Detroit Diesel, a company owned by General Motors, provides various diesel engines; gasoline-powered engines are obtained from Chevrolet. GMC also uses engines from Cummins and Caterpillar in situations where they would best meet the needs of specific trucks or custom trucking requirements. Transmissions for many GMC trucks are also provided by the Detroit Diesel/Allison division.

Another feature from GMC is the availability now of its new Dragfoiler, an aerodynamic mounting for the cab roof of most GMC heavy trucks. The Dragfoiler reduces wind resistance and therefore improves fuel economy. It was developed in the GMC labs and tested in wind tunnels and on the highway before being introduced in the mid-1970s. GMC officials say it produces some rather dramatic results: more than 20 percent fuel savings when used on a standard GMC Astro, for example.

More than 14,000 people are directly employed by GMC in the production and marketing of its heavy and medium trucks. GMC also maintains a network of 2700 sales and service outlets.

INTERNATIONAL

Young Cyrus McCormick began what was to become International Harvester back in 1831 when he built the first successful reaper, although the name and the company as we know it today did not actually come into being until 1902.

McCormick patented his invention and opened a Chicago factory in 1847 to produce it. The business grew and expanded in the United States, and went international in 1851 when McCormick introduced the reaper to England.

At the turn of the century, there were two major harvesting machinery manufacturers: McCormick Harvesting Machine Company and Deering Harvester Company, both in Chicago. The two companies merged, brought in three other smaller manufacturers and named the resulting firm the International Harvester Company. Cyrus H. McCormick Jr., son of the reaper's inventor, was elected the company's first president. International Harvester launched into the production of a large assortment of farm equipment, and the rest is history. Today, the company is known throughout the world and has total sales well in excess of $5 billion a year.

International Harvester's association with the agricultural industry led it into the truck business, to provide the farmer of the early 1900s with a method of transporting his produce to market in a way that was more efficient than horse carts. In 1907, the company introduced its "Auto Buggy," a wagon which was designed to look like a traditional horse-drawn buggy but used a two-cylinder engine

International's Transtar Eagle is a conventional model designed especially for the owner/operator.

International Transtar II cab-over-engine truck hauls a load of wood through the Alabama countryside.

International COF 4070B Transtar II.

Transtar Eagle cab-over-engine model.

for power. After that came the "Auto Wagon," only a little more trucklike than its predecessor.

World War I spurred the development of trucks, and International Harvester played a large part in it. After the war, International's truck manufacturing business continued to grow. By 1925, the company was the largest producer of a full line of trucks in the United States. In the early 1950s, International became the world's first company to mass-produce what was then a novel vehicle—the cab-over-engine, heavy-duty diesel truck. International Harvester now produces some 80,000 medium and heavy-duty trucks each year in seven principal lines, and is the largest manufacturer of heavy-duty

Model F-2674 with mixer body.

"Severe Service" S-Series F-2554 dump truck.

International's S-Series includes the model F-2575, which is often used by the petroleum industry to transport oil.

trucks. International also manufactures its own diesel engine, gasoline powerplants and many of its own transmissions and axles.

Its Transtar line of long-distance heavyweights is one of the most respected on the road today. It is offered either in a cab-over-engine model or conventional. Transtar trucks have the modern conveniences, power and contemporary engineering that are required for extended hauls. The new Transtar II Eagle was developed especially for owner/operators and offers an almost endless array of optional accessories.

If a true "all-purpose" truck were to be chosen from all makes and models, the new International

International's Low Front Entry model COF-5370 is designed to accommodate front-loading refuse trailers.

Harvester S-Series would have to be considered for the title. The company claims that there are 61 different occupations where S-Series trucks have definite application. This innovative line of trucks can be customized to accommodate a variety of bodies, from vans to ready-mix units and from tankers to dumpers. The conventional cab is comfortable and functional, and there are numerous options available with each of the many possible configurations.

Cargostar is another International Harvester cab-over-engine model, this one geared for medium to heavy jobs either in the city or between cities. The line can be tailored to open-road hauling, refuse disposal, flatbed adaptations and other functions. It is available with either diesel or gasoline power.

Another extremely versatile member of the International fleet is the Paystar. This rugged conventional can be found hauling materials or mixing concrete on construction sites, in the petroleum fields and anyplace where power and traction are important.

The Fleetstar, too, is a vehicle especially suited to construction work. It is a low-cost truck that is as much at home in the field as it is on a city street.

International Harvester's Loadstar is specially designed for a variety of city hauling jobs and refuse disposal. The new COF 5370 is another truck engineered to serve private and public hauling needs in urban areas, including the transport of consumer goods, refrigerated items, liquids and gases, and solid waste.

To produce the huge number of trucks it does, International Harvester maintains three plants at Fort Wayne, Indiana; Springfield, Ohio; and Chatham, Ontario. To sell and service the trucks produced, International has approximately 900 dealers and distributors for its mediums and another 800 to handle the bigger models.

International Harvester is truly international: its trucks are sold and serviced throughout the world.

S-Series F-2275 model with van trailer.

KENWORTH

Kenworth trucks, it could be said, grew out of the great forests and logging camps of the Pacific Northwest.

Early in the 20th century, the age of animal power was coming to an end: the horses and oxen that once dragged logs out of the woods under the whips of hard-driving bullpunchers were put to pasture. Rivers to float out timber were not always nearby or accessible. The forests had already begun to recede from the rail lines, and trains could not climb the steep grades encountered by loggers in the rugged terrain.

The solution to the forest industry's transportation problem was trucks. Trucks could maneuver along the muddy paths (in those days they could not legitimately be called roads), and climb hills four times steeper than the strongest locomotive could. The logging truck had to be incredibly strong, and its operator had to be both deft and heroic. The truck and driver faced grades so steep that the rig had to be hauled up by winch and then driven down fully loaded, along pathways of mud strewn with planks for traction. They faced landslides, flimsy wooden bridges and the constant fear of blowouts in the straining tires.

That is where Kenworth came into the picture. At the time when flappers were dancing the Charleston in city speakeasies, the Kenworth Motor Truck Corporation began making trucks to haul timber out of the forests of Oregon and Washington. From the one-model line of trucks manufactured in Seattle in 1923 by H. W. Kent and Edgar K. Worthington—who each contributed a syllable to the company's name—Kenworth grew to the giant it is today. The line now includes seven distinct models that cost anywhere from $40,000 to $75,000, depending on the number of optional accessories. Customized, specially constructed trucks can pass the $100,000 mark. Kenworth now turns out more than 10,000 trucks annually to travel the roads of the world.

Kenworth boasts—and rightfully so—that it has been a trend setter in the truck manufacturing industry. It maintains a long list of "firsts" in the field, such as:

- First six-cylinder gasoline engine factory installations
- First gas-turbine-powered truck in scheduled freight service
- First factory-installed aluminum diesel engine in a truck

Kenworth conventional with tanker.

Kenworth cab-over with van trailer.

Kenworth K100 cab-over-engine model.

Kenworth 548, a 50-ton dumper.

- First extruded aluminum frame
- First cab-beside-engine highway transport tractor
- First sleeper design with an aerodynamic roofline that acts as a fuel-saving wind deflector.

Kenworth has been producing commercial trucks for more than 50 years now, with the exception of the period during World War II when the company geared up to the war effort and directed its energies to the manufacture of a variety of military vehicles and bomber nose assemblies.

Kenworth still is a prime supplier of trucks to lumber and forest products businesses. Over the years, however, the company has expanded. It now provides vehicles to practically every branch of the heavy-truck transportation industry. Although Kenworth specializes in heavy-duty trucks, it is diversified enough within that class to turn out a range of vehicles from lightweight tractors for specialized needs to the true "heavies" with total truck, trailer and cargo weight of 600 tons.

Kenworth's current line of trucks includes the ultraluxurious cab-over Aerodyne, designed for long-distance driving. Its aerodynamic roof houses a 6'9" walk-in sleeper where anyone short of Wilt Chamberlain can stand up and stretch. Another top-line model from Kenworth is the V.I.T. It comes as a conventional luxury model with a walk-in sleeper, and as a cab-over model with a double bed. The Kenworth C-500 is an extra-strong, maneuverable vehicle that is especially suited to the logging, mining, construction, petroleum and refuse industries. Another Kenworth workhorse is the W-900, a versatile tractor that can be customized for many different purposes, from transporting tanks of milk to hauling herds of livestock. The

W-900 with timber trailer.

Kenworth V.I.T. conventional.

C-500 conventional chassis.

Kenworth's revolutionary Aerodyne.

Brute is an extremely rugged, on-highway construction truck. The Kenworth 548 combines strength and durability in a bruiser of a 50-ton hauler. Kenworth also makes Gliders, so-called kits for rebuilding wrecked or outdated trucks. Gliders normally include a new cab, and front axle frame and accessories; the buyer provides the engine, transmission, rear axle and suspension system.

All Kenworth trucks are fully equipped and offer a large variety of standard features and options including refrigerators, air conditioners, color televisions and plush interiors with walnut dashboards that would bring a grin to the face of a limousine owner.

Over the years, Kenworth has been especially proud of its dedication to driver comfort. During the days of bone-jarring trucking in the 1920s, Kenworth was the first to put four-inch-thick pad-

ding under the trucker's bottom. Today's amenities include deluxe upholstered air-ride seats, deep-pile nylon carpeting, double beds or bunk beds on some models, walls and ceiling of tufted upholstery, stereo systems, reading lamps and other comforts of home.

Kenworth, which employs about 2500 people and enjoys annual gross earnings of half a billion dollars, is still headquartered in Seattle. Today, however, it is a division of PACCAR, a large diversified transportation company, and Kenworth trucks now roll off assembly lines in seven plants: Seattle; Kansas City, Missouri; Chillicothe, Ohio; Vancouver, British Columbia; Montreal, Quebec; Mexicali, Mexico; and Victoria, Australia. Kenworth maintains a distributor organization throughout the world, with more than 100 distributors in the continental United States alone.

The Kenworth V.I.T. conventional is the most luxurious conventional model in the company's entire lineup.

31

MACK

Mack is to trucks as Coke is to cola and Kleenex is to facial tissues. The phrase "Built like a Mack truck"—now a copyrighted corporate slogan—has for decades been a familiar figure of speech in the United States. The company's hometown calls itself the "truck capital of the world." The burly bulldog that sits atop each Mack truck is as well known as the Flying Lady who graces the hood of a Rolls-Royce.

Few companies have acquired this kind of recognition. Mack has been so honored because it has been around so long and has earned an excellent reputation for its line of dependable vehicles.

The Allies depended on Mack trucks during World War I. In the war years, Mack exported various tough-looking haulers to Europe to move heavy artillery and other military gear. British troops dubbed the snub-nosed trucks "Bulldog Macks," and the bulldog became a trademark of the company in 1932. Mack trucks have traveled the battlefields of every war in which the U.S. has been involved, from World War I to Vietnam.

John M. "Jack" Mack founded the company in 1900 in Brooklyn, New York. Five years later he moved the firm to Allentown, Pennsylvania, where it has been ever since. In the early days of the business, Mack built buses, rail cars and trolleys as well as trucks. In recent years, however, the company has focused its full attention on the manufacture of heavy trucks and their powertrains.

A list of "firsts" for Mack would be a long one: the firm's numerous advances in truck design and engineering are well known throughout the industry. Mack is so large today that its assembly lines can turn out about 26,000 trucks each year. Its annual sales figure is bigger than $1 billion. Mack is now a subsidiary of The Signal Companies, Inc., one of the United States' largest corporations.

Mack's big conventionals are powerful enough to haul doubles—two trailers full of heavy cargo.

Mack conventional for toughest jobs.

Mack U Series with offset cab.

In the fleet of Mack trucks on the market today, there is a heavy-duty vehicle for almost every transportation purpose. The Cruise-Liner is a handsome new truck from Mack that is called "one of the lightest, if not *the* lightest" cab-over-engine models in the heavy-duty, long-distance hauling industry. It was engineered with traditional Mack performance in mind and with a contemporary concern for fuel economy. The Cruise-Liner offers many modern conveniences and comforts with an ample supply of optional accessories.

The Interstater is another cab-over-engine model for long hauls. The FL is a third cab-over that is light and specially geared for use in the mountains and deserts of the American West. The Mack MB, on the other hand, is a short-haul, intercity truck that is ideally suited for maneuvering in congested urban areas.

Mack refers to its conventional line of heavy trucks as "the true workhorses of the highway," and they are built to accomodate either medium or long-distance hauling requirements. The Mack R

One of Mack's rugged cab-over-engine tractors hauls a double load of livestock down the highway.

Cruise-Liner is a big Mack COE.

has been a respected hauler of massive loads for years. The Mack RD, with its great reserves of power, can handle even bigger loads—the toughest assignments to be found in heavy-duty trucking. Where outstanding traction is required, the Mack RM is called into action. It is specially designed for use with snow plows and has performed well under the most severe conditions.

The RL is Mack's lightweight conventional, a cousin of the cab-over-engine FL lightweight. The RL is designed to handle the steep grades and rugged, extended hauls that a trucker can encounter in the mountains, forests and flatlands of the West and the Pacific Northwest.

The U series of conventional truck models pro-

vides an offset cab, designed for better visibility. The design is unique and symbolic of Mack's inventiveness in the heavy-duty truck field.

The DM is Mack's construction truck. It can be customized to carry dumpers, mixers, refuse units, bulldozers and construction shovels.

Mack manufactures its own engine and transmission systems at a special plant in Maryland for use in its trucks. The Mack powertrain is installed in most of the company's vehicles, but Mack also uses engines from other makers such as Cummins, Detroit Diesel and Caterpillar. There is an easy way to tell whether a Mack truck has a Mack engine, just by looking at the vehicle's grille. If the bulldog on the hood is gold, the engine is Mack's; if it is chrome, the engine is from another manufacturer.

Mack's Maxidyne engine and Maxitorque transmission were introduced in 1966 and were hailed as the most significant breakthroughs in diesel technology in 15 years. The transmission employed only five forward speeds (six for some extremely heavy-duty haulers) instead of the ten to fifteen speeds of regular gearboxes. The Mack transmission offered the trucker a 65 percent reduction in highway shifting, and provided more usable horsepower and torque than any other powertrain then in production. The Maxidyne 300 engine, a six-cylinder powerplant, was significant in the way in which it minimized engine cooling requirements.

Mack maintains a huge plant and its corporate headquarters at Allentown, but the company also has truck manufacturing facilities at a number of other locations in the United States and Canada. It employs more than 15,000 people to produce and sell these trucks with the bulldog on the front. Mack also maintains more than 800 sales, parts and service centers in the United States and Canada that are supplied by a master parts warehouse in Bridgewater, New Jersey. The entire operation is linked by a satellite communications system, a product of space-age technology and the revolutionary concepts that Mack has fostered throughout its history.

Mack truck with concrete mixer.

Ruggedly built Mack RM 600.

Color
Convoy

Today's big rig works hard, but not without style. It is an imposing combination of power and elegance befitting a true king.

AUTOCAR

There is no such thing as a regular production Autocar truck, according to company officials. Each Autocar is custom-built by a division of White Motor Corporation.

CHEVROLET

Chevrolet's heavy-duty truck line includes the Bison (top), a conventional-cab design that is built to withstand the strain of long-distance transport of heavy cargo. For jobs requiring less power over shorter distances, Chevrolet markets a line of medium-duty trucks including the C65 (bottom).

Chevy's new Bruin(top), introduced in late 1977, is similar in many ways to the Bison(bottom), but features a completely new interior with improved driver headroom, shoulder room and hip room. The windshield area is large to allow greater visibility. The front end of the Bruin is made of fiberglass to reduce weight.

CRANE CARRIER CORPORATION (CCC)

The Centurion cab-over is one of the big rigs in Crane's line. It is available with or without sleeper. The wide expanse of glass provides the driver with great visibility in all directions. Numerous interior and exterior options are available to enhance appearance and comfort.

The Centurion cab (top) features a low-profile design that makes it suitable for specialized tasks such as refuse operations using front loaders.
Crane's Centaur (bottom), which is famous for durability, is a conventional design that is in wide use in foreign countries.

The Centurion (top) is available with several brilliant color schemes.
A third cab style in the Crane line is the Century (bottom), with a single-passenger cab
that is especially well suited to the short-haul needs of the construction industry.
The Century is often equipped with concrete mixers, cranes and large dump trailers.

FORD

The big trucks from Ford include the CL-9000 (top), a cab-over truck available in three different cab lengths from the 54-inch "shorty" to the 110-inch family sleeper. The conventional selection includes the L-Liner series (bottom) which also is offered in several cab sizes and hauling capacities.

Other Ford conventionals with short cabs are the L-Line 800 (top) and the
F-800 (bottom), rigs which perform well in all medium-duty applications. The smaller cab
size increases maneuverability, making the 800s adaptable to varied
types of commercial cargo hauling.

FREIGHTLINER

Trucks from Freightliner are available in conventional (top) and cab-over types. Each features a comfortable sleeping area. Components used in both of the models are made of aluminum alloys to reduce weight and improve efficiency. Freightliner offers a wide range of interior materials.

Freightliner's conventional (top) and cab-over provide the driver with a high level of luxury and comfort. Sleeping compartments are available in several sizes, while vinyl, velvet and leather upholstery can be ordered. Custom paint, chrome and other options can be had by truckers who want to customize the interior of their vehicles.

FREIGHTLINER

The Conventional is the newest member of the Freightliner family.
The company has put more than 80,000 heavy-duty trucks on the roads of North America
in the past ten years and is one of the leading producers of big rigs.

FWD

FWD is a maker of several special-purpose trucks. The line includes the
FWD C-60530 concrete mixer and other trucks equipped for snow removal, municipal
utilities installation and the construction trades.

GMC

The General (top) leads GMC's truck parade. Its conventional-cab rig is well suited to all types of heavy tasks. One of GMC's smaller trucks is the Steel Tilt cab-over (bottom), which boasts good maneuverability — a factor that is important when the job requires trucking through heavy city traffic.

Many of GMC's smaller conventionals (top) are in wide use by businesses such as landscaping services. The Brigadier (bottom) is shorter than the big General, but also handles heavy jobs. It features a fiberglass front end that increases durability, makes maintenance easier, and also helps to reduce weight.

The General (top) is as much at home on the highway for long-distance chores as it is in transport of heavy cargo for shorter distances. GMC's short conventional line includes several models designated 97.5 — the number of inches from the front bumper to the back of the cab. They are available in several tonnage ranges.

INTERNATIONAL

International says its Western Paystar 5000 SF (top) has been trimmed of 1000 pounds through the use of lightweight construction materials, without a sacrifice in strength. Smaller than the Paystar but strong enough for big loads of sand and gravel is the International Loadstar (bottom), called the "Little Giant."

A Class 8 cab-over from International is the Transtar II (top), brawny enough for the biggest payloads. Interiors of International's big trucks are equipped for comfort, easy accessibility to controls and good looks (bottom).

Other major movers in the International line include the Transtar (top), capable
of hauling the heaviest loads over long distances; and the S-Series of powerful trucks
designed for cargo transport over shorter distances (bottom).

KENWORTH

Everything you would need to build a truck, except the drivetrain and rear supension, is included in the Kenworth Brute Glider "kit" (top). The Kenworth W-900 (bottom) is a complete truck — not a kit — that offers the trucker a high level of interior comfort and the muscle to move loads of 20 tons and more.

KENWORTH

For truckers who may need a new cab for a busted-up truck and who likes the looks of the
W-900, Kenworth sells a W-900 Glider kit (top). Another mammoth truck in
the Kenworth line is the C-500, an all-business machine that can easily handle tons of
sand and gravel and other tough assignments.

Kenworth trucks like the W-900 (top) and the Brute (bottom) are hard at work for the petroleum industry and the construction trades. They carry concrete to the site of major construction projects and haul thousands of gallons of petroleum products across the North American continent to heat those new buildings.

Kenworth V.I.T. cab-over is the choice of many husband-and-wife trucking teams, because of its luxurious interior features including diamond-tufted upholstery, full-length clothes closet and double-size bed. The V.I.T. line includes deluxe conventional models as well as cab-over designs.

MACK

New in the Mack line for 1978 is the Super-Liner (top), designed to meet the special needs of truckers who own and operate their own rigs. The wraparound instrument console makes for easy monitoring of the rig's operations. The cab-over Cruise-Liner (bottom right) features a spacious sleeping compartment.

MACK

The Cruise-Liner cab is light in weight, and this allows for greater payloads. The cab is large and comfortable, suited to the needs of the long-distance driver.

MERCEDES-BENZ

Mercedes-Benz, German producer of luxury sedans, is also heavily into the truck manufacturing business. One of its models in use in the United States is the L1113 diesel.

OSHKOSH

Many of the bigger rigs from Oshkosh (top) have been modified slightly and are now in use by the U.S. Army as heavy equipment transporters. The Oshkosh M-1500 (bottom) plays an important role in airport safety. It was designed to provide fire protection with a capacity of 1500 gallons of water and 180 gallons of foam.

Other big rigs from Oshkosh (top) feature all-wheel drive for outstanding traction required by the construction trades. Many other Oshkosh trucks are depended upon to keep major roadways free of snow (bottom) and are equipped with special snow-removal accessories.

Oshkosh builds the P-3 series of trucks to serve individuals and businesses in America's snow belt. They are specifically designed to keep things moving, no matter how harsh the weather. The company is also a major supplier of aircraft tow vehicles for the United States Air Force (bottom).

PETERBILT

Whether the rig is a conventional (top) or a cab-over (bottom), Peterbilt rigs are tough enough to take the most difficult hauling assignments in stride. Materials used in the construction of Peterbilt dumpers must be especially strong to withstand the heavy load requirements and harsh conditions of the construction site.

PETERBILT

Hauling doubles is what it's called. It means you have two huge trailers — a load that can be a strain for all but the toughest rigs. Some Peterbilt trucks are especially designed for this type of punishing work. And when the job requires an overnight stay, Peterbilts with sleepers ensure a good night's rest.

SPARTAN

Spartan's HH-1000 is a diesel-powered heavy hauler that is equipped to handle the most rigorous kinds of hauling duties. An HH-1000 is currently in use in the coal fields of Virginia, where it hauls 40 tons of coal with each trip.

VOLVO

Volvo's F86 cab-over diesel (top) has been engineered to meet the requirements of intercity commerce in the United States. The cab is especially roomy for a rig of this size. Another Volvo product, the F613 (bottom) features a form-fitting driver's seat that was designed to reduce fatigue on the long haul. The cab is especially strong.

WALTER

Walter trucks are designed to meet specialized needs. The Walter II, for instance (top), is a cab-over design that is used for snow removal and other road maintenance work. The Walter "C" crash rescue vehicle, with 3000-gallon water capacity, is used at airports to put out fires.

WHITE / WESTERN STAR

The White Western Star (top) is a conventional design that is tough enough
to handle the most difficult hauling assignments. Custom paint jobs with as many as
12 different colors are available. White's Road Xpeditor 2 (bottom), with cab-over
design, features the same toughness.

In addition to the wide choice of interior appointments and exterior colors, White's Western Star (top) can be ordered with a variety of engine and drivetrain combinations to suit particular jobs. The Road Boss 2 (bottom), which was introduced recently after six years of development, is new in the White lineup.

MERCEDES-BENZ

It seems appropriate that Mercedes-Benz, maker of some of the most expensive luxury sedans in the world, also manufactures trucks to transport money. On the other hand, it seems ironic that this elegant and distinguished name can be seen on trucks that haul garbage. But Mercedes-Benz is as involved with one as much as the other, manufacturing armored cars as well as heavy-duty refuse disposal trucks.

Mercedes-Benz is a grand old name in automotive history. The company was founded by the two men who are credited with inventing the internal-combustion automobile: Carl Benz and Gottlieb Daimler. The first Mercedes automobile was designed in Germany back in 1900, several years before the first Ford Model A was built. Trucks were later brought into the Mercedes-Benz line, and the company eventually grew to be the world's largest manufacturer of trucks over 12 tons and the largest producer of diesel-engine trucks.

Despite this long tradition, Mercedes-Benz is a newcomer to the United States truck market. A Mercedes truck was not test-marketed in the U.S. until the late 1960s. A full marketing program was not instituted until 1970, and only 150 Mercedes-Benz trucks were sold in America that year. The German company now sells more than 1100 trucks each year in the U.S., and sales are growing.

Large trucks from Mercedes-Benz like the L1316 are used by many fuel companies in America as delivery vehicles.

Presently, there are three Mercedes-Benz trucks on the American market: two medium-size Class 6 models, the L113 and the L116; and the light-heavyweight L1316. Besides money and garbage, these trucks are capable of transporting a vast assortment of items and materials around the cities and suburbs of the United States because they are highly adaptable vehicles, produced with urban needs in mind.

Mercedes-Benz uses diesel engines in its medium and "lighter than heavy" trucks sold in America. Although diesel engines are now available in domestic automobiles and trucks, the diesel was not widely used in small trucks in the U.S. when the first Mercedes models were imported. For that reason, Mercedes-Benz has conducted a program in the United States which is intended to educate the American truck buyer in the benefits of diesel power. The key word that Mercedes officials use to describe their diesel engine is performance. According to the company, diesel performance means better mileage; fewer repairs, and therefore less down-time; and longer engine life. In addition, Mercedes officials say ever-increasing gasoline prices will prompt truck owners and operators to seriously consider the diesel.

The largest of the Mercedes-Benz trucks moving on American roads today, the L1316, has the same cab and powerplant as the two smaller Mercedes models; but it has a stronger frame, heavier axles and springs, and a larger cargo capacity. The L1316 is ideally suited to intercity shipping services, beverage and fuel oil delivery, and refuse collection. The L1316 comes in four wheelbase sizes and costs from $18,500 to more than $20,000, depending on the options selected and the point of delivery.

The two smaller Mercedes-Benz trucks, the L1113 and L1116, are often called "sister trucks": they are basically the same, with the only major difference being that the L1116 turbocharged engine generates 156 horsepower and the L1113 engine provides only 130 horsepower. Both trucks incorporate the sophisticated engineering that is part of the Mercedes-Benz reputation, and are available in four wheelbases. Mercedes claims that these diesel trucks provide up to twice the mileage of similar gasoline models and have a shorter turning radius than any comparable truck. These trucks cost $15,000 to $18,000.

Mercedes-Benz trucks exported to America are manufactured at a huge, ultramodern facility in Sao Paolo, Brazil. Mercedes-Benz trucks, buses, parts and components are also produced at other plants in England, Australia and the Middle East. Almost 50,000 trucks and buses are produced annually by Mercedes-Benz and shipped to many countries around the world. More than 16,400 workers are employed to do the job.

The United States is only a small part of the world truck market for Mercedes-Benz. With continually growing sales and an expanding dealer network, however, Mercedes-Benz has definite plans to take a larger portion of the medium and light-heavyweight truck market in North America.

Mercedes L1316 chassis.

Mercedes-Benz armored car.

Mercedes L1113s equipped for sanitation work.

OSHKOSH

Oshkosh builds some of the most unusual vehicles currently manufactured in the United States. It produces trucks specially designed to drive across broiling deserts, to plow snow and ice in the worst of winter, to put out intense fires at the scene of an airplane crash, to haul army tanks and other heavy military equipment, and to carry huge concrete mixers wherever they are needed.

The Oshkosh company's vast central plant is situated in Oshkosh, Wisconsin, an area where most of the industrial activity revolves around paper and dairy products, and where much of the talk is about fishing, snowmobiling and the Green Bay

Packers. It has been the home of Oshkosh Truck Corporation ever since the company was founded back in 1917.

The firm was started by two Wisconsin residents, B. A. Mosling and William Besserdich. Besserdich had helped to launch the FWD Company, another truck manufacturer, nine years earlier. In the years that led up to World War II, Oshkosh concentrated on manufacturing all-wheel-drive vehicles for use primarily in highway construction, heavy-duty hauling and snow removal. The business grew and the company broadened its line, but it remained in Oshkosh.

Many big Oshkosh trucks are used by the United States military to haul tanks and other armored vehicles.

The firm's employees have traditionally come from the city of Oshkosh and the surrounding towns and rural areas. Several generations of some families have earned their livings in the Oshkosh truck plants. The trucks assembled by those workers can be found in practically all areas of the United States and in many foreign countries.

An Oshkosh aircraft rescue truck is stationed at the home base of the Royal Australian Air Force, a model J tows disabled vehicles out of the sands of Saudi Arabia and an Oshkosh E-1223 has been converted for bus service in South Africa. An Oshkosh Desert Prince loads up in Pakistan with supplies for oil drilling sites, and an Oshkosh F carries concrete along the Alaskan pipeline. Surprising as it might seem, an Oshkosh P-3 snow removal truck travels the roads of Iran.

The company makes the world's largest airport fire truck. The gargantuan M series fire-fighting unit has a capacity of 6000 gallons of water and more than 500 gallons of foam concentrate. Its pumping capacity is 2000 gallons a minute. This giant vehicle can move loads weighing up to 125,000 pounds. Each of the vehicle's eight tires stands six feet tall, and the eight tires contain as much rubber as 232 standard automobile tires. Its twin engines can generate as much as 860 horsepower. This extraordinary vehicle is now in service at airports in the United States and abroad.

The L series of fire fighters is also unique. It includes the lowest vehicle made by Oshkosh, a truck with a chassis that measures only six feet from the ground to the top of the cab. The Oshkosh L is designed so that ladders and snorkel systems can be mounted on top and still clear low viaducts and the entrances of older firehouses.

The U.S. Army in 1976 asked the Oshkosh company and other major truck manufacturers to bid on producing an extra-strong specialty truck for transport of the army's main battle tank, which weighs in at well over 50 tons. The vehicle the Army wanted was one that could run at 43 miles an hour with a total load of 95 tons. The tank carrier also would have to be able to move that load up a 3 percent grade at 14 miles an hour and be capable of starting and operating with that same weight

Oshkosh F-3 Series truck with mixer.

Oshkosh P series truck with snow plow blades.

Oshkosh L-1838 fire truck.

B Series Oshkosh with concrete mixer.

Oshkosh P series truck with dump body.

M6000 airport crash/rescue vehicle.

Huge Oshkosh rigs like the Desert Prince are built to withstand the strains of the very toughest types of hauling jobs.

while on a 20 percent grade. It would have to be able to function in temperature extremes from 125 degrees Fahrenheit to 25 degrees below zero. There were many more requirements, and the Oshkosh design met them all: its F-2365 is now in production for the army.

Oshkosh also makes regular trucks for more common tasks. The E series, Oshkosh's cab-over-engine models, are large, heavy-duty haulers for the open road. The F series vehicles are con-struction trucks, adaptable to many kinds of con-struction needs from hauling concrete mixers to carrying dump-truck beds. The P series trucks from Oshkosh are all-wheel-drive vehicles with excellent traction that are widely used for snow removal. Oshkosh's B trucks are relatively new, designed to be customized to meet a variety of construction needs. Oshkosh R models, conventionally styled trucks, move lumber and other weighty cargo on highways and dirt roads.

PETERBILT

In the depths of the worst depression in the history of the United States, September of 1934, Al Peterman drove his Cadillac into the small, poverty-stricken town of Morton, Washington. Many of Peterman's associates in those days described him with such adjectives as energetic, dynamic and inventive. The 750 residents of Morton, who were wondering where their next meal would come from, did not use glowing terms to describe the newcomer in the expensive car.

Elsewhere in the state, Peterman owned a lum-bermill and a few vehicles which he had modified and converted into logging trucks. What he needed was timber. The area around Morton had good timber and Peterman had the means of getting it from there to his mill. So, he set up a logging operation in Morton and hired more than 100 townspeople to work it—almost 15 percent of the town's citizenry. Morton's people began thinking about the man with the Cadillac in a much friendlier way.

Peterman's timber business grew until it could

Peterbilt makes a line of cab-over-engine rigs that are especially suited to the needs of the long-distance trucker.

Peterbilt cab-over model with sleeper.

Conventional for construction hauling.

no longer be adequately supported by his small fleet of modified logging trucks. To live up to his reputation as energetic and inventive, perhaps, he decided to build his own trucks, rather than to buy them from a truck manufacturer. In 1939, he bought the Fageol Truck & Coach Company of Oakland, California. He quickly changed the name to Peterbilt and directed the company's activities toward the production of vehicles for his logging operations.

Peterman was not content with just a single line of trucks. He began to expand the line with other types that he found his company capable of building. Peterman recognized that he was fully in the transportation business: the truck company was no longer just a supplier to his logging activities. He began experimenting with a number of different truck configurations, including a chain-drive vehicle for use in the sugar cane fields of Hawaii. When the United States entered World War II, Peterbilt produced trucks for civilian use as well as for military purposes under various contracts from the U.S. government.

Al Peterman died in 1947. The company, enjoying sales of $4.5 million by that time, was bought by its employees. Still growing 11 years later, Peterbilt was purchased by PACCAR, a huge corporation in the transportation industry. (PACCAR also owns Kenworth Truck Company, a major manufacturer of heavy-duty trucks which also got its start in timber hauling.)

Over the years, Peterbilt acquired a good name in the business. The company presently makes a variety of heavy trucks for long-distance transport and some specialized vehicles for the construction, logging and mining industries.

To haul freight over long distances, Peterbilt manufactures cab-over-engine models as well as conventional trucks. A deluxe COE, the Peterbilt 110, has a cab and double sleeper that are luxuriously outfitted with padded vinyl upholstery. Other cab-overs are specially designed by Peterbilt engineers for the tough task of hauling two trailers at a time, including flatbeds, vans, tankers and bottom dumps. The lightweight 282 and the heavyweight 352 are strong enough to haul doubles with ease.

Peterbilt also makes a conventional model that is especially well suited to the needs of truckers who haul tankers. Another Peterbilt conventional is customized to serve the logging industry. It is a vehicle that evolved from the first Peterbilt truck of 1939, and is as much at home on the open highway as it is up in the logging hills. There is a conventional from Peterbilt that is made to take on the toughest types of construction hauling—double loads, dump-truck operations and off-highway maneuvers. Rugged Peterbilt trucks used with concrete mixers are available in a number of models.

All told, Peterbilt has a line of 14 different truck models, each with great potential for customization. All are noted for performance and special attention to driver comfort and convenience. One of Peterbilt's significant contributions to the industry is the "Air Trac" suspension system, which increases comfort and cuts vibration.

Peterbilt currently has a work force of more than 2000 people. Each year, the company manufactures about 13,000 trucks. There are 122 Peterbilt sales and service centers, and two primary manufacturing locations: Newark, California, and Madison, Tennessee. In addition, the company is building a mammoth plant in Denton, Texas, which is expected to begin operations in late 1979.

Peterbilt has come a long way since that day when Al Peterman drove into Morton looking for timber.

SPARTAN

Spartan Motors of Charlotte, Michigan, is just now getting its tires on the ground. The company was incorporated in 1975 and began turning out heavy trucks the following year.

The people of Spartan Motors are not new to the truck-building industry: about 95 percent of the firm's present workforce are veterans of Diamond Reo, a truck company that for many years was owned by White Motor Corporation. Reo was started in the early 1900s by Ransom E. Olds, who is better remembered for developing the Oldsmobile car. When Diamond Reo was sold by White and subsequently was liquidated a few years ago, a number of Diamond Reo management and factory employees went in together and founded Spartan. Thus a new name entered the highly competitive arena of heavy-truck manufacturing. (Diamond Reo trucks are now being manufactured by Osterlund, Inc., of Harrisburg, Pennsylvania.)

Spartan Motors is the smallest of the manufacturers discussed in this chapter, both in terms of the number of trucks it produces and its sales volume, but its growth record is outstanding: its output has increased by 100 percent in its second year of operation. That impressive rate of growth is related to the company's small size and modest beginnings, but it is also an intimation of the way the fledgling company could expand in the future.

Spartan builds specialized vehicles. A company spokesman says Spartan is in the business of helping customers who are "looking for special, custom-type units and who could use some help in solving some very special needs." To that end, the company is organized to provide direct and close personal assistance to customers in designing custom trucks.

So far, the company has produced its 2000 series of truck, a cab-over-engine vehicle that is versatile enough to serve as a hauler or a fire truck. The brand new HH-1000 is a rugged diesel with a gross vehicle weight up to 140,000 pounds (depending on the application and tire size). The HH-1000 was tested out by moving 40 tons of coal per trip over a six-mile course with an 8 percent grade in the rugged terrain of West Virginia's coal fields. Spartan also manufactures some highly specialized derrick trucks used by utilities to dig post holes.

The young truck company makes many of its own parts and components and obtains others from various manufacturers.

In developing a reputation for quality-crafted vehicles, Spartan has utilized the talents of experienced truck builders. The company has already shown a great potential for growth and the ability to satisfy the needs of a specific segment of the truck market. In its two years, Spartan has provided proof that there is room for the small specialty producer and customizer in an industry dominated by giants.

Spartan's CFV-2000 cargo tractor.

CFC-2000 fire truck from Spartan.

VOLVO

Volvo is a true industrial titan, employing 62,500 people in Sweden—roughly 2 percent of that nation's entire population. Headquartered in Gothenburg, which is a seaport, a major industrial center and Sweden's second-largest city, Volvo makes cars, trucks, buses, tractors, forestry equipment and hydraulics and recreational products. The yearly sales of this vast corporation, the largest manufacturing company in all of Scandinavia, total $3.5 billion. Volvo exports more than two-thirds of its annual output, to 160 countries around the world.

One of those countries is the United States, where Volvo automobiles have acquired a reputation for high quality and durability. Volvo cars have been available in the U.S. for a number of years, but it was not until 1975 that the company decided to introduce its line of trucks to America. That does not mean Volvo is a recent entrant in the truck manufacturing field. On the contrary, the company has been manufacturing heavy-duty trucks since 1928. Volvo is now the fifth largest maker of heavy-duty diesel trucks in the world, producing more than 21,500 trucks each year. It also manufactures its own engines, transmissions and most of the other major components and accessories for its trucks.

Its U.S. reputation for quality automobiles and its success with trucks in other parts of the world prompted Volvo to enter the highly competitive American truck manufacturing field.

A new truck division was created and brought under the control of Volvo of America, which markets all Volvo products in the United States. Volvo of America now has 750 employees and is headquartered at Rockleigh, New Jersey; the truck division, however, makes its home about two miles away in Northvale, New Jersey.

In 1975, its first year of sales operation, Volvo sold only 36 trucks in the U.S.; the following year, the number of units sold jumped to 150; the 1977 sales figure is about 500 units.

Volvo came to the American truck market with only one vehicle, its F86. It is a versatile Class 8, cab-over-engine model that can handle both medium and heavy trucking chores—interstate highway hauling as well as intercity delivery. The F86 uses a six-cylinder, turbocharged Volvo diesel engine and an eight-speed, synchronized Volvo transmission. According to the company, this vehicle is a fuel saver that can average up to 10.5 miles per gallon.

Volvo introduced a new truck, the F613, to the American market in the summer of 1977. This cab-over-engine model is intended for short hauls and is designed to minimize the difficulties of maneuvering trucks along city streets. Two years of road tests were conducted on the vehicle before it was released to either the European or American market. Volvo says the F613 is highly adaptable and can accommodate a platform body, a van body with a lift gate, a beverage van body, a refrigerated van, a fuel or chemical tanker or a refuse collection unit. The F613 also was built to provide good fuel economy. It is powered by a 170 horsepower, turbocharged diesel engine produced by Volvo.

Volvo's current network of about 50 dealers covers only 15 states along the East Coast of the U.S., from Maine to Virginia. Expansion into the Midwest is expected to get under way soon.

Volvo trucks have made giant strides during their first few years in America. If the company's accomplishments with trucks turn out to be anything like what it has achieved in the U.S. automobile market, Volvo will be extraordinarily successful on the American truck scene.

Volvo model F86.

WALTER

In this day and age, it is difficult to imagine a company manufacturing automobiles in the heart of New York City, out of a plant on 65th Street just west of Central Park. But that in fact is where the Walter Motor Truck Company began.

Back in 1898, William Walter developed the Walter car and began turning the cars out of his small factory in Manhattan. By 1905, production was up to 300 vehicles a year—a sizable amount in those days when horse-drawn carriages were just barely being nudged off city streets and Henry Ford was still eight years away from introducing assembly-line mass production.

In 1911, Walter decided to move into other automotive areas. Trucks seemed to be the coming thing, he decided, and that was the direction in which he steered the Walter Automobile Company. That year, he changed the company name to the Walter Motor Truck Company and produced his first heavy truck for special hauling purposes. Over the years, the Walter company has kept that name and maintained the original goal of producing special-purpose heavy-duty trucks.

The early Walter trucks utilized revolutionary technology such as electric drive and air suspension, and they were accepted as important contributions to the development of the truck as a sophisticated and adaptable machine.

After World War I, people at Walter became aware of the need for four-wheel-drive vehicles. They knew how effective such trucks had been in the mud and snow of European battlefields. They realized that this type of truck could be used efficiently on American roads, at construction sites, and in forest and mining areas which were growing rapidly in many areas of the United States. It was then that the Walter 4-Point Positive Drive was developed. This now-famous system employed the principles of suspended double-reduction drive axles, equal weight distribution, correct four-wheel-drive differential action and an automatic lock to prevent wheel spin when traction was lost.

Throughout the years, as Walter continued to refine and improve these hardy vehicles, special attention was paid to the design of airport maintenance and emergency trucks. Special Walter trucks move snow off runways, fight fires and transport first-aid teams to the scenes of aircraft accidents. Beginning its efforts shortly after World War II, the company has developed some of the most highly respected vehicles in the field.

The Walter CBC 3000, a twin-engine fire fighter, has a capacity of 3000 gallons of water and 500 gallons of foam concentrate. It is used at major airports around the world. Smaller fire fighters like the BDQ 1500 and the CFR are built for use at smaller airports.

Other Walter 4-Point Positive Drive units remove snow from highways and city streets; haul municipal waste and landfill; pull concrete mixers and cranes; tote equipment used in digging tunnels; travel to dam sites; and service the lumber, mining and construction industries.

More than 300 employees work to produce Walter's rugged vehicles at the company's main plant in Voorheesville, New York.

Walter Snow Fighter.

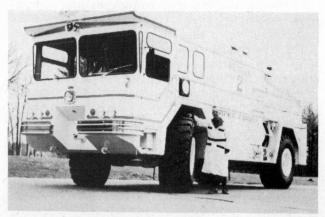

Walter C Model rescue truck.

WHITE/AUTOCAR

Thomas H. White started his little sewing machine company in New England the year after the Civil War ended. It is unlikely he ever imagined that the modest operation would grow to become a corporate giant with annual sales well over $1 billion, but his was one of those companies that was destined to grow. Some 30 years later, Tom White's three sons decided that it would be a good idea to expand into a burgeoning new field—automobile manufacturing. In 1900, the White brothers built their first steam-powered car and truck.

By 1906, the automotive division of the White company was booming. It was separated completely from the firm's continuing sewing machine operations, and that was the beginning of White Motor Corporation as an independent manufacturer of motor vehicles.

During World War I, White produced military vehicles for both the United States and France. When the war ended, White gave up automobile production and concentrated all its efforts on the manufacture of trucks. World War II pushed the company back into military production, and White turned out a large assortment of military trucks and half-tracks that rumbled over battlefields as far apart as the Ardennes Forest in Europe and the Solomon Islands in the Pacific.

The two decades after the war were a period of acquisition and diversification for White. In the 1950s, White bought three truck manufacturers: Autocar, Reo and Diamond T (the latter two were sold in 1971 and both subsequently went bankrupt). In the '60s, White expanded into the farm equipment industry, which, like the truck operation before it, would grow into a multimillion-dollar operation for the company.

Over the years, White Motor Corporation became a dominant force in the transportation field. The

White Western Star with tanker trailer hauls thousands of gallons of liquid cargo down the highway.

White Road Boss 2.

White Road Xpeditor 2 with refuse body.

White's brawny Road Boss.

Road Commander 2 cab-over.

name White became synonymous with well-made trucks, and it maintained a well-earned reputation for product dependability and ingenuity. Autocar, for example, was responsible for developing the porcelain spark plug; White was the first company to develop and produce the power-tilt cab.

In 1951, White took over all sales and service operations for Freightliner, which would also become a giant in the truck manufacturing world. White handled these functions until 1977, when Freightliner went back to handling its own sales and service.

Currently, about 10,000 people work for White Motor Corporation in truck manufacturing, sales and service. More than 20,000 trucks are sold each year by White, and gross annual revenue from the sale of these trucks is more than three-quarters of a billion dollars. White now manufactures trucks under three nameplates—White, Autocar and Western Star—in a wide variety of models and types to serve the divers segments of the heavy-duty truck market.

Several new models were added to the White line recently, as the company worked to fill the gap left when Freightliner operations departed. To produce these new trucks, White built a huge new plant outside of Roanoke, Virginia. It covers more than 400,000 square feet and is capable of turning out a complete truck every ten hours.

One of the new White trucks is the Road Commander 2, a cab-over model that is aerodynamically designed to be an efficient and economical long-distance hauler. Inside and outside, the Road Commander 2 is sleek and modern in anyone's terms.

The Road Xpeditor 2, another new White model, is especially suited to the needs of the short-haul trucker. It is designed primarily for delivery service and refuse collection in urban areas. The interior is comfortable, and more than 400 options are available.

White's Road Boss 2 is a strong, durable conventional truck model. Introduced in 1976, it features many modern amenities and up-to-date engineering.

The White Western Star line of trucks has its roots in the logging industry, where the toughest of trucks were needed, and Western Star still serves that industry with distinction. Western Star trucks serve a wide variety of other transportation needs as well.

The other White nameplate, Autocar, is a totally customized construction truck—one that White refers to as a "hard-working, no-nonsense truck." Autocar trucks often can be seen hauling construction equipment, a wide range of construction materials and huge concrete mixers.

As it grew over the years, White Motor Corporation moved from New England to Cleveland to its present home in Eastlake, Ohio. Instead of the tiny shop where sewing machines once were assembled by hand, White now has six mammoth truck manufacturing plants. Besides the new Virginia facility, there are plants in Cleveland, Ohio; Exton, Pennsylvania; Ogden, Utah; Kelowna, British Columbia; and Brisbane, Australia.

In the White corporate family, there are divisions that manufacture farm and industrial tractors, harvest combines and other farm implements, off-highway haulers, coal haulers and fork-lift trucks.

Western Star with load of timber.

Road Boss 2 tractor.

White's big Road Commander 2.

Custom-built Autocar from White.

BEHIND THE DRIVER

Behind the driver of a powerful tractor headed for a road construction site are two Trailmobile aggregate trailers.

In the tractor or the cab of a truck are the driver and the powerplant; behind it are the goods, the cargo, the payload—the truck's real reason for being. Whether it is a van filled with the belongings of a family moving cross-country, an air force flatbed gently taking a missile to its underground launch pad, a fire engine rushing its sophisticated pumping equipment and life-saving gear to the scene of a fire, or a garbage truck making its daily rounds, each vehicle has special duties and is specially customized to serve them.

There is such a vast and varying amount of merchandise, raw materials and other items of cargo to be moved that it would be impossible to show all the kinds of trailer customizations that are now on the road. But even a brief review is a tribute to the

adaptability and effectiveness of the truck as a key means of transportation.

In the beginning, truck manufacturers had a limited vision of the truck and its potential. It was first looked upon as a motorized wagon that could be used in the cities to move only small quantities of merchandise. Its greatest contribution, many people believed, would be its replacement of the horse cart as a city delivery vehicle and the clean streets that would result. For the farmer, it would be interchangeable as a hauler of his goods and a carriage for his family.

It did not take long, however, for pioneers in the field of truck manufacturing to see that their inventions could do much more. Nor did it take long for commercial establishments to suggest what

Refrigerated van from Great Dane is designed to haul perishables over long distances.

Weld Built is one of several companies that specialize in the modification of trucks for use as wreckers.

kinds of trucks they wanted. Manufacturers were quick to respond.

It is amazing to chart the truck's development over the years and to list the various functions that trucks handle today. It is not easy to categorize them, because some fit no particular category and others overlap into several different groups. A heavy-duty tractor/trailer hauling gravel could be classed as an interstate hauler, a construction vehicle, or even a military vehicle, depending upon who it is working for and where it is going.

The open-road convoy of interstate trac-tor/trailers includes many kinds of enormous rigs that have become a common sight on highways across the country. There is no way that anyone could make an all-inclusive list of the things they carry. Construction vehicles are grouped together because they usually work as a fleet. They build highways, housing developments and city skyscrapers; they tear down outdated buildings and tear up worn-out roads. Industrial vehicles are truly specialized to work the logging camps, mines and oil drilling sites. Some are equipped with sophisticated and powerful cranes and drills; others have

Fruehauf makes temperature-controlled tankers that are used to transport resins, paraffin and asphalt.

Hydraulic dump trailer from Fruehauf, made of aluminum or steel, uses a "bathtub" design for high strength.

special hauling capabilities.

Tankers have their own unique characteristics and requirements. Fire fighters need specific equipment to meet a variety of emergencies in cities and rural areas. All branches of the armed services require specialty vehicles to carry troops, haul supplies, move tanks from factory to fort, and transport fuel across an airfield.

The cities need public and private vehicles to keep things moving, from manufacturers to stores and from stores to the customers' homes.

The payload carrier, that highly adaptable container riding behind the truck driver, is what enables the truck to do all of these things.

Flatbed trailer from Fruehauf can be adapted to carry a large variety of very heavy materials.

Another type of trailer for hauling construction materials is the Nordic Bulker by Trailmobile.